KELLY HOPPEN

MONOCHROME HOME

Rizzoli
NEW YORK

Text by Helen Chislett   Photography by Thomas Stewart

KELLY HOPPEN

MONOCHROME HOME

HARMONY, BALANCE, AND THE ELEMENTS OF MODERN STYLE

to friends

CONTENTS

FOREWORD

The idea of producing a book that zooms in close, rather than taking the conventional broad picture, was an exciting concept to me. Firstly, it reflects my own philosophy that each view within a room, no matter how small, is important. Often it is not the big decisions that make the difference between mediocre and superlative design, but the attention to detailing. Choosing an upholstery material, for example, is only the beginning when dressing a chair. Thinking about stitching, piping, introducing textural contrast through cushions, or deciding on the perfect backdrop is what transforms that chair into a focal point.

I also wanted to convey the sense of movement in a room, the fact that an interior is not static. It is human nature to become bored, be it with our clothes or our homes. It may not be practical to redecorate every few months, but it is possible to regenerate a space by moving, exchanging, or altering some components within it. *Monochrome Home* is full of such ideas. It shows you how to look at a room and really see it; how to focus on each individual object; and how to keep a space alive and organic.

I have enjoyed working on this book more than I could ever have envisaged, partly because putting my style under a magnifying lens has given me a different perspective on my work. The pictures are a joy; but do find time to read the text also, because it is like a bridge between what the eye sees and how the mind plans. There are no rules here. What I hope is that by seeing how I work, you can take my ideas and translate them into your own decorative style. Anything goes; the rarely admitted secret of decorating is that anything will work if it works for you. The integral part of design is understanding who you are and how you want to live.

This book is a gift from me to you. May it bring you much pleasure.

THE KELLY HOPPEN SIGNATURE

This book—a look through the zoom lens at what I do—provides a perfect opportunity to explain what my work is all about. Magazines and newspapers often dub me a minimalist. In fact, although I admire the minimalists and have learned a great deal from them—the way in which they interpret a space is cleaner and clearer than anybody's—I am not, and never have been, a minimalist. My own style is actually warm rather than stark, luxurious rather than ascetic, and organic rather than static. I like to begin with a space that is very structured and edited, but then to inject it with warmth and comfort. The unexpected way I juxtapose textures, objects, or shapes within a room underpins much of what I do, but would be interpreted by a true minimalist as positively frivolous. Whereas a minimalist keeps the lines of a room etched sharply across a space, I like to begin with those same lines but then blur them at the edges.

When designing, I work on instinct alone—never really stopping to think about why something works or how a room comes together. This book is an invitation to step inside my head and to see what I see when I look at an interior. Space is obviously the first consideration, but many people think of a space as something to be filled. I believe that first you have to understand the space—its physical properties, the strength and direction of light within it, and its interplay with adjacent spaces. It is also essential to relate it to the people who will be using it and how they will be using it.

When it comes to positioning furniture and other objects within a space, it is important not to fill it so tightly that movement is restricted. That word "movement" relates not just to being able to walk around in comfort, but also to movement of the eye. Allowing a certain amount of space between individual items gives a room a sense of flow, which is calming. Don't punctuate the space with too many ingredients, or it will have the awkwardness of a badly composed sentence.

The way I assemble a room in my head is by imagining it on a three-dimensional grid system. Structure is crucial to my work, so this linear interpretation of how a space works is invaluable. However, it also overflows into other aspects of my design life: runners, rows, banding, or panels also stress this geometric approach, a way of imposing order onto previously disharmonious interiors.

However, once the core design is in place, my natural tendency is to look for ways of shaking it up. A room that is overdisciplined is in danger of becoming boring, so I like to introduce a touch of excitement—

something contrived to catch the eye. This is quite a subtle technique; it would be completely against my philosophy to introduce anything garish or vulgar just for its own sake. It might be that I place a very small-scaled object adjacent to a large one; a group of identical, symmetrically placed items alongside one asymmetrical piece; or, perhaps, a free, organic shape against a rigid man-made one. Texture also offers opportunities to make these visual plays. The mix of matte and glossy, rough and smooth, clear and opaque all contributes to the visual success of a room. Teaming a very humble fabric, such as felt or terry cloth, with something lavish, like silk or taffeta, is a particularly pleasing way of overlaying that sense of interest.

I am absolutely passionate about detail. Everything I introduce into a room must have a sense of harmony. To me, it makes no sense at all to redecorate or refurnish a room and then ignore the way the cushions are stacked, flowers arranged, or objects displayed. All the time that I am contemplating such details, I am considering them on two levels: the individual vista I am creating and how that relates to the backdrop of the room itself. Nothing should be overlooked, whether it is the way candies are arranged in a dish or photographs on a shelf.

I am also driven by a desire to bring atmosphere and mood into a home. Good artificial lighting is obviously a key component here, but so are scent, taste, music, and touch. A home should wrap itself around you, so you feel completely warm, safe, and cocooned. It is not enough that it looks fabulous; it must feel wonderful, too. Remember also that although a home should be a sanctuary, it is never isolated from the environment outside. A strong influence in achieving visual and tactile comfort lies in reflecting what is happening in the seasons. The gray days of winter need a different treatment from the airiness of summer or the sharpness of spring.

Finally, much of what I do is about stepping out of the ordinary. People assume that everything I use must be expensive. In fact, though, I love taking modest household objects and transforming them into chic additions to a home, with a little bit of lateral thinking. Baking trays, mixing bowls, and lids of boxes are just a few of the examples you will find here. But remember that everything shown is intended to be a springboard for your own ideas. Once you have had a chance to look at my signature, it is time to think about creating one of your own.

ABOVE Even the smallest of objects can be arranged with care to add a layer of beauty to a room. Here, the opaque, milky surface of eggs has been highlighted by a black lacquer plate. This allows one texture to play against another and is also an example of how the repetition of simple forms can create a still-life composition.

OPPOSITE Consider, too, the backdrop to an arrangement. Here, ornate, creamy marble has been enhanced with a contemporary runner of polished plaster. The use of small-scale items—three ceramic bowls—adds an unexpected twist to a traditional fireplace. Their asymmetrical positioning also draws the eye, instead of allowing it to rest more conventionally at the center of the mantelpiece.

RIGHT Rooms should never be designed in isolation, but should relate to those around them. Here, the view from the dining room looks through to the hallway, where three tall wenge tables have been placed alongside each other to replicate a conventional console. Twists of tightly packed snake-grass in round glass bowls on each one emphasize their height. Wenge has also been chosen for the dining table, with dark-edged picture frames above echoing its tones.

PAGE 16 One fabulously textured object can create a focal point within a room. This carved wooden artifact has a fascinating ridged surface which contrasts perfectly with the simple glass bowl and velvety chocolate cosmos.

PAGE 17 Fabric is another way of bringing a textural highlight to a room. This pleated, chocolate Fortuny silk flows to the floor as if it were liquid. Dark-stained floorboards create a dramatic backdrop.

PAGE 18 The same fabric can now be seen in full, used to cover a hallway chair. Behind is a striking black-and-white photograph of actress Glenn Close, which has been positioned to create impact as visitors walk in.

PAGE 19 Rooms should taste as delicious as they look. Feed the senses by displaying food seductively. Here, a silver dish on an antique Chinese table makes the perfect foil for chocolate-covered coffee beans.

SPACES SEEN AND UNSEEN

The golden rule I always try to make people understand is that to transform your home you must be able to see not only objects but the space between objects. A space, to me, is as important visually as a fabric or a table. It is part of the balance of the room and must be considered on an aesthetic level.

As with anything else, it can be analyzed on varying scales. If you are designing a whole room, it is best to empty it of everything so you can rub out your mental picture of it. Think about its shape, proportions, and architecture. Note the position of doors, windows, and fireplace. Now try mentally to dissolve the walls, so you can see how this room leads into other spaces within the house and how each space relates to the next. Do not rush this process. Spend as much time as you need simply looking and contemplating. Play music that you love, and allow yourself to become immersed in your thoughts. The idea is to expand your mind so that you can see all the possibilities for a room, rather than becoming entrenched in how it is now.

The beauty of learning to look at space is that this technique can be applied to small cameos as well as large areas. Perhaps this is not the moment to redecorate on a grand scale. Instead, it might be that you want to revitalize your home, rather than completely transforming it. Concentrating on creating pleasing still lifes around a room can train the eye just as effectively.

Decide on the corner you want to rejuvenate, such as a mantelpiece, side table, or alcove. Empty it—no matter how much you love the objects usually displayed. Pack everything in boxes, and put them out of sight for at least six months. They will make a reappearance in your life at some point in the future, but nothing should remain static—least of all a home.

Now consider that area in terms of color, texture, and lighting. These are the means by which you are going to make a canvas on which to paint, metaphorically speaking. Look at the textures that are there, such as the smoothness of marble or the richness of wood. Now think how you might emphasize these qualities by introducing objects with a contrasting surface. Once you have found your inspiration, it might be a question of using items you already own but placing them in a new setting, or buying something with this space specifically in mind. When positioning them, however, remember to keep looking at the space, not just at what you are putting into it. Be critical; take as long as you wish to move things around, introducing or discarding certain elements until you have created something that is in balance with its surroundings. The more you concentrate on the small vistas of a room, the easier it becomes to change the bigger picture.

You must also have an awareness of the importance of spaces never usually seen: the insides of cabinets and drawers, for example. Order is so important to our mental well-being that it is not enough merely to pay it lip service by applying it to what is on display. It should be evident throughout an interior—and that includes those seldom-seen places. Opening a flatware drawer to find everything immaculately stored and ready for use is just as uplifting as opening a door to find a room arranged with care and intelligence.

When looking at the space as a whole, you should first reflect on its physical boundaries. You also need to develop an awareness of the natural light. Work with the light you have before making decisions about incorporating the artificial kind. If you were building a house on a plot of land, the first thing you would do is calculate where the sun rises and sets. That, in turn, would help you to decide on the position and outlook of rooms. In a house that is already built, you still need to know how light falls at different times of the day and the year. How else will you know where best to position furniture? Just as the space between objects is as important as the objects themselves, so shadows are as beautiful as light. Once you know how light moves, you can decide whether you want it to flow into the room uninterrupted or would like to filter it or diffuse it to create interesting effects of light and dark. It is not until you have fully comprehended the natural light in your home that you can make decisions about the artificial kind. The latter is not only for use by night. It can also boost gray days, throw attention onto a particular tableau, or become a decorative form in its own right.

The room may still be empty, but now you must imagine filling it with furniture, objects, and textures. Don't lose sight of the space itself. Remember, this is as important as all the decorative items you plan to introduce. Once you have an image in your mind, you could transfer these thoughts to a storyboard. Create a montage of inspirational pictures, color samples, fabric swatches, and sketches to see how the room would look.

Now is the time for a moment of honesty. Does the picture you have created correspond to the type of person you are? Do you have the discipline not only to create the look, but to live in it? This is not a showpiece, but your home. You have to feel comfortable with it, just as you have to feel at ease in the clothes you wear or the car you drive. Think about how you live and the people who live with you. Lifestyle is the most important ingredient, and it must be at one with the space.

ABOVE AND OPPOSITE The dining room seen on pages 14–15 has now been set for dinner. Although the basic components of wenge table and Alcantara-covered chairs remain unchanged, a transformation has been achieved through linen, tableware, and accessories. The picture opposite shows a bird's-eye view of the place settings with taupe, deep purple, and lilac plates, combining to produce a mood conducive to nocturnal dining. Wineglasses also are pale amethyst. Taupe linen napkins and a linen runner placed lengthwise on the table create a visual link to the chairs and the draperies behind. Silver glasses placed along the center in a row are the perfect containers for tea lights, which create a soft glow in keeping with the subdued color scheme.

ABOVE It is not necessary when decorating to lavish money on every item, but it does create an impact if you choose one or two objects to turn into eye-catching focal points. These antique chairs from Paris are covered in lush suede and have been further enhanced by purple silk runners and silk cushions. The result is luxurious and seductive, an invitation to relax into a cocoon of opulent fabrics.

OPPOSITE A completely different space for day or night can be created by using walls that are fluid, rather than solid. Here, runners of different fabrics—sheers, silks, even leather—are hung the height of the room and can be changed according to the desired mood. Used by night, as shown here, they create a dramatic setting for a dinner party. Rich purple glasses, a satin runner, glass plates, and napkins made of three different silks combine to give a backdrop to a Bacchanalian feast.

OPPOSITE PAGE A close-up of the dining room shown previously focuses the eye on the raw silk of the dining chairs and the way in which this blends with the banner-style runners hung along the walls. This use of fabric emphasizes the soft boundaries of the room and creates an atmosphere that is truly inviting.

BELOW LEFT The classic lines of this Mies van der Rohe stool have been emphasized by the soft swathe of a cashmere throw. This makes an interesting contrast to the curved stainless-steel legs and white leather upholstery. A coir floor adds another textural dimension.

ABOVE RIGHT The shape of a wenge-inserted panel in a row of bedroom wardrobes has been echoed here by the positioning of two cotton runners over a mohair bedspread, with appliquéd satin rectangles. The linen pillow covers continue the geometric theme with appliquéd satin squares.

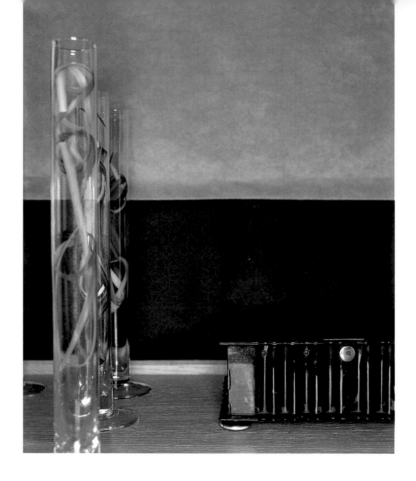

ABOVE Taupe suede has been combined with dark green wool to create a smart Roman shade for a dressing room. The sheen of the tortoiseshell box makes a pleasing contrast to the matte of the suede. Three tall jars filled with curling iris leaves make an unexpected departure from a conventional floral arrangement.

OPPOSITE Touches of color can be used to create subtle visual links within a room, pulling the eye from place to place. Here, the red wool of the cushion on a suede chair echoes that of the mango calla lily in the glass bowl. Twines of pussy willow also pick out the wenge and ivory of the lamp set behind the wenge table.

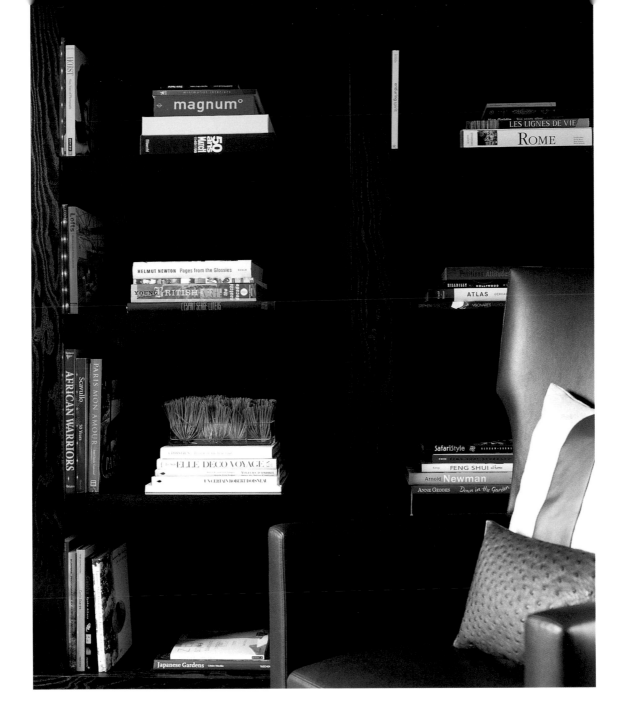

OPPOSITE Texture is also an effective way of bringing all the strands in a scheme together. This bird's-eye view looks down on a wooden floor and silk carpet bound with chocolate-brown leather. Leather has also been chosen for the chair upholstery and as a band over the linen back cushion. A small chocolate-brown ostrich cushion finishes off the composition to spectacular effect.

ABOVE An upright view of the same chair shows how each ingredient balances with the others. Set against wenge shelving filled with books, it creates a quiet area within the room. The positioning of books has been given the same consideration as that of any other object—note how they have been assembled according to scale, proportion, and color. Fiber-optic lighting set into the unit edges adds interest without disturbing the tranquil mood.

This elegant living room has been arranged so that the shape of each object interplays with those around it. Note how the horizontal line of the wooden coffee table is echoed by the slats of the seat back, and how the pedestal table in the background has a scaled-down reflection in the lamp on the floor. The dark wenge of the chair has been complemented by rich red leather upholstery and a sumptuous red horsehair cushion. Textural harmony continues with the bound linen rug and linen draperies. A collection of amethyst-colored glass on the table makes the perfect backdrop for fiery red clove carnations, a jolt of color in a monochrome room.

From a different angle, it is now possible to see that the living room is in fact on mezzanine level and looks down onto the dining room shown on page 25. Here you can see the full impact of ceiling-to-floor panels in linen and leather viewed over the balcony of toughened glass. These vertical lines have a strong influence on the scheme and are picked up throughout the room. The wenge chair with horsehair cushion is now seen from the front, providing a link to the lamps and tables behind. The whole composition is extremely sophisticated, right down to the glass balustrades of the staircase, the Chinese lacquer boxes, and the Kelly Hoppen rugs.

OPPOSITE A close-up of one of the Kelly Hoppen rugs shown on the previous page, with the distressed lacquer coffee table and parquet floor, illustrates how strong linear pattern is within a scheme. Using two contrasting colors emphasizes their graphic quality.

ABOVE The cube shapes of sugary Turkish delight have been echoed here by a geometric arrangement on a slab of square slate. The spaces between each one have been considered as carefully as those of a permanent still life within a room.

SYMMETRY AND ASYMMETRY

Because the linear dimension is so important to me, it is natural to embrace symmetry in design. Symmetry impresses order onto a space, and that is something I value very much. Just as understanding space is a question of seeing the space between objects, so arranging an interior is about recognizing the relationship between objects. Form, scale, texture, and color all give clues as to how best to achieve harmony in a scheme.

At its most obvious, symmetry is about taking two or more identical objects and placing them close to each other for maximum visual impact. It is one of the unfailing techniques of decorating and is apparent in interiors ranging from English country houses to New York loft spaces. However, it has other interpretations, too, such as repeating a shape in different scales. This could include, for example, different-sized pillows layered one onto the other, or a collection of identical vases ranging from low to high. Although this is not symmetry in its strictest sense, it has the same effect in an interior of emphasizing structure and form. Finally, it can be about arranging furniture and objects in a symmetrical manner. This might be achieved through the way chairs and tables are positioned, how pictures are hung, the arrangements on shelves or mantelpieces, or through very geometrical window treatments. It can be achieved either through the juxtaposition of perfectly balanced objects or by teaming up objects that, although not identical, have corresponding qualities that link them together. It might be the way a painting echoes the shape of a fireplace, for example, or how a lampshade reflects the form of a cabinet.

Whatever the approach, for symmetry to retain its force, everything in a room must be carefully edited. If there is too much going on in terms of color, pattern, or extraneous objects, the eye will be distracted. Instead, you must strive to be as disciplined as possible about what is on display, so that attention is naturally focused on the area you wish to highlight.

Whereas symmetry is fairly easily understood, asymmetry is often overlooked. An asymmetrical arrangement might include one object that bears no obvious relation to those surrounding it. It might, on the other hand, include identical objects that are positioned in an asymmetrical way. Like symmetry, it is a powerful instrument in design, particularly when used in conjunction with a symmetrical arrangement. The stark contrast between one and the other is a way of throwing each into sharp relief. If you find this hard to comprehend, consider how textures are used in interiors. If you choose something rich for draperies, such as silk, there is little point in teaming it with something equally opulent—taffeta, say—because the textures will merge together. Instead you might choose to put silk with something humble, such as scrim or felt. The contrast will delight the eye and sense of touch, and will allow both materials to be appreciated fully.

So it is with symmetry and asymmetry. Start with your symmetrical arrangement, and then place something close to it off center. This will punctuate the space and inject some excitement into the design. It might be a question of using one tall object, so that height becomes a factor. It might be that you introduce an organic shape against a line of regimented ones. It could be that instead of hanging pictures in rows, you lean them against a wall with each frame overlapping.

Carry this idea one step further by thinking about how you might arrange identical objects in an asymmetrical way. Take a mantelpiece arrangement as an example. The traditional way of dressing one is to have a centerpiece of some description—perhaps a clock—and then to lead out from each side of this with symmetrical arrangements of candlesticks, photo frames, lamps, vases of flowers, ornaments, or any other decorative extras. But let us say you placed a pair of lamps at one end of the mantel and a clay figure at the other, with nothing else between but a simple row of single banana leaves in tumblers, each positioned to point in the same direction. Attention would still be drawn to the clay figure, even though it is not center stage or surrounded by symmetry. In fact this would be a far more dynamic arrangement than the conventional kind, because symmetry and asymmetry would be working together to achieve something unpredictable and visually stimulating.

This is important, because good design is about avoiding the obvious. Just as combining textures is about finding contrast, so arranging objects is about considering the conventional treatment first and then looking for ways to turn this on its head. Remember this next time you are creating a still life of objects, be it on open shelves, a side table, or a mantelpiece or in an alcove. It is not that success is guaranteed—be prepared for several attempts before finding the one you like—but that taking a fresh eye to any situation is a way of engendering inspiration. Once you begin to analyze the qualities that symmetry and asymmetry bring to a room, you will have fun discovering what powerful tools they can be.

OPPOSITE When considering each view within a room, think carefully about how every object affects those around it. The organic shape of this Arne Jacobsen chair makes an interesting play against the rigidity of a floating shelf. The symmetry of three identical glass vases, each holding a single red dahlia, is reduced by placing them asymmetrically at one end of the shelf. Overlapping photo frames in different sizes also place symmetry and asymmetry in tandem and contribute to the balance of the total effect.

ABOVE Consider the vertical dimension also when creating interesting vistas. The elongated light hung above this Perspex table is an unexpected contrast to the broadness of the Vietnamese lacquer vase filled with Bordeaux dahlias. The vibrant red of these is picked up in the red velvet runner placed over the table, bringing an exciting rush of color to an otherwise calm scheme.

ABOVE LEFT A bed is like a canvas on which you can paint colors and textures. Here, an ostrich leather headboard is complemented by crisp white linen, a red velvet runner, Chinese rattan headrests, a long striped silk pillow, and a satin eiderdown. The result is a blend of wonderful textural contrasts and a perfectly balanced composition.

ABOVE RIGHT A separate view of the room featured on page 32 shows the wenge chairs on one side of the room and the creamy velvet upholstery on the other. Red cushions on each act as a visual bridge, with dark glassware and crimson flowers punctuating the space.

OPPOSITE A close-up of the wenge chair shows the printed red leather upholstery and horsehair cushion, which bring a layer of richness to the scheme. Just one fabulous texture, such as the horsehair, can be enough to bring a whole room to life.

OPPOSITE Objects work particularly well when arranged in groups of three, five, or seven; often even numbers result in an oversymmetrical format. Here, wooden cylinders from Africa create an unusual still life, with a single cocoa leaf for impact. The rough concrete floor is a good foil to the richness of the wood.

PAGE 44 Collections of nonidentical but similar objects also work well visually. Here, shagreen boxes of different sizes create a pleasing still life against an antique mirror. Reflected in this is a French *chaise longue* and sculptural lamp, while in the foreground a silver bottle laid over the boxes adds another decorative touch.

PAGE 45 Pillows of different sizes look particularly appealing when made of varying textures but similar colors. Here Alcantara suedes, velvets, and silks in various finishes complement each other, while contrasting well with the textured wall behind.

OPPOSITE This perfectly harmonized composition draws together the key components of height, scale, texture, and interest. The wenge cabinet and leather lamp set the style, but it is the sculptural shape of papyrus in a vase lined with cocoa leaves, juxtaposed with the unusual subject matter of the photograph, that determines the mood. The inclusion of small objects emphasizes the large scale of the vase, while two pencils have been placed in the horn beaker to reflect the number of ceramic bowls close by.

ABOVE This cool living room illustrates the beauty of the monochrome scheme. The dark-stained wooden floor has been balanced by a simple cream rug bordered with leather. A tall wenge lamp and wenge sofa base echo the floor tones, but the linen shade, pale-colored upholstery, and sheer curtains act as a foil to these. In place of the conventional coffee table, a banquette has been used. This can double as additional seating or be used as a surface for trays of drinks or flowers, such as the green papyrus shown here. Cushions in suede, linen, and leather are stacked to emphasize the ordered atmosphere.

OPPOSITE The colors and textures of food can be key players in creating a delicious still life. Here vegetable chips have been placed in a wooden bowl, which catches the light around its rim.

ABOVE In this dining area of a kitchen, a wenge table has been teamed with banquette seating and chocolate-brown chairs, all upholstered in linen with a plastic finish so that they can be wiped clean easily. Sticks of snake-grass cut to fit the dimensions of a wooden bowl are a simple but effective centerpiece, while others have been placed in simple glass vases just behind the banquette. An old kitchen clock adds character.

ABOVE One of the most enjoyable approaches to design is to take a conventional idea and give it a twist. Here, for example, instead of one large mirror above a wenge console table, a pair of wenge-framed mirrors have been used. These, in turn, reflect the wenge cabinets at the other end of the room. The graphic lines of this arrangement have been emphasized by the symmetrically placed pair of lamps and the collection of silver teapots in gradations of scale.

OPPOSITE A close-up of one wenge cabinet shows how a similar subtle change of scale has been used to draw attention to the individual Moroccan ceramic bowls displayed here. Cleverly designed lighting within adds an extra layer of interest and is enhanced by the wenge lamp to the right. The pale-colored shade of this echoes the creaminess of the china.

ABOVE Here the mirror over the fireplace is a contemporary interpretation of a traditional juxtaposition. It is as though the fireplace had a removable central panel which has been lifted out and placed above, so exactly does one shape fit into the other. The square table echoes this effect, while antique amethyst-colored rummers are set off center to blur the rigidity of the lines.

BELOW Cushions with geometric panels and borders impose a sense of order upon surroundings. Here they emphasize the form of the headboard, which is upholstered in oxblood and camel cotton.

OPPOSITE Fiber-optic lighting on the edges of open shelves is a clever way of giving definition to a quiet area.

OPPOSITE A different view of the living room shown on page 47 demonstrates how the introduction of one strong color can alter the mood of a room. Here an orange pashmina makes a luxurious throw; it could also be used as a band around a cushion. Replacing the green papyrus with an arrangement of kumquats emphasizes this dynamic effect.

ABOVE Long loaves of bread are tied with rope for added textural definition. Placed on a simple polished concrete table against a limestone floor, they make an unusual still life.

PAGE 56 A bird's-eye view of the kumquats seen opposite shows them laid in a Perspex box, placed on a wooden tray on the linen-upholstered banquette. The one spectacular mango calla lily on top not only accentuates the power of the color but creates an interesting asymmetrical effect against the carefully arranged rows of fruit.

PAGE 57 Choose pictures that complement the scale of their surroundings. This striking photograph of Marilyn Monroe is a strong image which perfectly combines with the very graphic modern fireplace. The orange cross scratched over the image adds another layer of interest to a bedroom that is otherwise monochrome.

PAGE 60 Scale is a key player in this contemporary bedroom. The huge mirror leaning against the wall matches the scale of the door. In its reflection can be seen a wenge panel and wardrobe doors. The shape of the television adds to the graphic strength of the room. On the floor, the organic shape of two ceramic eggs throws the angular arrangement into relief.

PAGE 61 Black picture frames are complemented here by wenge rails on which to hang clothes.

OPPOSITE When used in a group of three, these tall wenge tables replicate a traditional console table in a hallway. Tightly packed bunches of snake-grass in glass bowls emphasize their vertical lines.

ABOVE Rows of identical objects are an effective way of accentuating the linear; here Perspex boxes of moss in white sand displayed on a linen runner create an unusual alternative to a conventional floral arrangement.

SEASONAL LIVING

For those of us who live in places where the seasons roll on, it is important to design homes that can reflect the altered state between summer and winter. The idea of dressing a house seasonally is not new, but it is true to say that it is increasing in popularity as people become more confident about creating homes that really work for them. Apart from visual considerations, this is, more importantly, a very practical thing to do. Your home should make you feel comfortable at all times. Part of that comfort is not feeling too hot or too cold, and this comes down to more than installing the correct heating system. It is about what floors feel like underfoot, whether upholstery fabrics are pleasant to the touch, and how much light there is in a room. Different things make us feel comfortable at different times of the year; that is what seasonal decorating is concerned with and why it should be thought about on many levels.

If you keep colors minimal, it is possible to achieve changes through more subtle textural variations. First, consider window treatments. If privacy is not an issue, you may not need draperies, curtains, blinds, or shades at the height of summer. If you do want some protection from the outside world, think of gossamer-light sheers or semi-translucent unlined curtains. In winter, you may need something to prevent the cold air from outside circulating through your home, but this can be achieved easily with internal shutters or double glazing. It is not necessary to hang heavy draperies, which will allow in even less light than usual. The Shoji panels I designed were inspired by my own need to pay homage to the change in seasonal light, without sacrificing the feel-good factor in my own home. Now I can transform my interiors by hanging leather or linen one day, suede or scrim the next. I have even included a Perspex variation for a truly purist approach. Not only do the panels make excellent window treatments, but they can also be used as room dividers.

Thinking about how the windows are dressed is only the start. Probably the most important consideration is how best to boost natural light when the days shorten. Any lighting scheme you install should be designed for daytime winter use as well as the obvious nocturnal one. Mini spotlights and flexible fiber-optic lighting are both excellent ways of introducing illumination and interest to a room—an additional layer of light that has both a functional and a decorative purpose.

If you design with the seasons in mind, you might also think about how to keep floors cool underfoot in summer and warm in winter. A simple way of doing this is to lay two layers of flooring: something solid, such as wood or stone, over which rugs or matting can be placed. Changes in temperature can then be reflected effortlessly by removing or replacing the top layer.

You should also think about how you use a room in winter, as opposed to summer. You might want to position furniture slightly differently, perhaps drawing seating closer together for a more intimate mood. Warmer months are often synonymous with living half inside and half in the garden. Open doors and windows extend the feeling of space, so that interiors become airier than in winter. If you keep major pieces of furniture, such as sofas and beds, fairly neutral, it is then possible to transform them completely according to the season, through textured items such as cushions and runners. Winter might be signified by red velvet runners on the table, a mohair throw on the bed, or charcoal felt cushions on the sofa. In summer, white satin runners, plain linen sheets, and cashmere cushions might be the order of the day. Think about investing in some items that can be used all year round, such as reversible throws in two contrasting fabrics.

Smaller, more portable pieces of furniture offer an additional way of recognizing seasonal differences. Transparent, semi-transparent, and highly polished materials, such as glass, Perspex, and metal, reflect or refract light and make an ideal addition to summer rooms. Winter might call for more solidity and stronger color, so wood or lacquer might be a better choice. Tables and occasional chairs, which can be exchanged according to season, are just as important as smaller accessories, such as vases or fruit bowls.

Flowers are the ideal way of reflecting changes in the seasons, as well as being one of the easiest ways to inject color. Think of the fiery red of autumn dahlias, as opposed to the pure white of summer lilies, for example. Flowers are also a way of bringing scent into a home, and scent, like colors and textures, should always be in tune with the seasons. But flowers are not the only way of introducing nature into the home: simple arrangements, such as winter twigs in white sand, can serve as equally pleasing focal points.

Finally, build up a collection of objects that you love for their decorative qualities. Consciously divide these into winter or summer displays. Pack them away until the right time of year, so that you are continually changing the small items in a room as well as the large ones. This will prevent the interior from becoming static, and you will enjoy rediscovering them anew every six months or so.

ABOVE Crisp white linen sheets and pillowcases create ripples against a headboard upholstered in creamy ostrich leather. The luxurious qualities of the latter set the signature of the room, but other textures can be changed according to season or mood.

OPPOSITE Ostrich leather has also been chosen for the elegant Roman shade in the same bedroom. A sheer curtain has been hung in front, which contrasts in both texture and the direction of stripes.

PAGE 66 A shelf unit of leather and wood has a back panel of lit milk glass, which creates an evocative backdrop to silhouettes of coral in a bronze pot. The simplicity of the arrangement allows the filigree-fine texture of the coral to be appreciated fully.

PAGE 67 Textured silver wallpaper and a Perspex box of white sand create a wintry setting for bleached dogwood twigs gathered from the garden.

OPPOSITE Ivory-colored dahlias make a dramatic centerpiece when gathered into a large Perspex box—the perfect addition to an airy summer scheme.

PAGE 70 The concrete bed base and concrete floor are given textural definition by the addition of a white satin runner.

PAGE 71 Viewed here through a Perspex panel, all of the components—from the concrete base and ostrich headboard to the white dahlias and Perspex furniture—combine to create a room that is cool, calm, and considered.

ABOVE LEFT Kelly Hoppen fabric in a variety of stripes has been used here to cover the headboard, duvet cover, and pillowcases in soft taupes and creams.

ABOVE RIGHT A floating shelf makes an almost invisible backdrop for identical glass vases, each holding a single cream 'Bianca' rose. Submerging the buds in this way accentuates the contemporary look.

OPPOSITE The floor and walls of this wet room are limestone, which not only is practical but brings natural beauty to the room.

PAGE 76 Mohair and fake polar bear throws on a cotton chenille bedspread are carefully folded to create a quiet still life. The small pillows are linen in envelopes of sheer.

PAGE 77 Translucent linen curtains fall to the floor, creating waves of light and dark against a plain wool carpet.

ABOVE LEFT Broad bands of contrasting-colored fabric on cushions and draperies accentuate the linear design of this harmonious room. Here the vertical of one plays against the horizontal of the other to interesting effect. Textural contrast is apparent in the use of cashmere wool against suede and unbleached muslin. Even the way the fabric falls sends out ripples against the floor.

ABOVE RIGHT Cushions do not have to relate to function, but can be used visually to layer a look. These include a combination of satin and chenille and look so delicious they are almost edible. Stacked on a velour-covered ottoman, they add height to this corner of the room, so balancing other elements of the scheme. When the ottoman is in use, the cushions can be put aside.

ABOVE LEFT The surface of a wall can be left undecorated without remaining blank. Here a pitted plaster-effect paint finish introduces texture for beauty and interest. Increasingly, surfaces such as this are designed to be inviting to the fingers as well as to the eyes. The juxtaposition of a contrasting texture, such as the silk and linen of these curtains, emphasizes this effect.

ABOVE RIGHT Much is made in decorating texts of the importance of light within a room. However, shadow can be just as mood-enhancing. The reading lamp here is positioned to throw light onto the crewelwork upholstery, but it also casts a half-light upon the clay figure standing on the wenge radiator case, etching it against the surface of the wall to dramatic effect.

STILL-LIFE COMPOSITIONS

Central to the enjoyment of a room is visual comfort—it must please the eye in order for the body and mind to relax. I give just as much attention to the way cushions are stacked or flowers arranged as I do to wall treatments or styles of furniture. For me, the effect of a beautifully designed scheme would be ruined if there were even the smallest note of disharmony. Still-life compositions are not just about the obvious, such as how a coffee table might be arranged. They are about paying attention to every vista in a space.

Think first about what you see when you first walk into a particular room. Is there an opportunity to introduce a focal point of some description—perhaps one fabulous piece of furniture or eye-catching work of art? There is no point having a centerpiece like this unless you are going to lavish attention on it, so consider its height, shape, color, and texture. Now look for ways of making the most of these, perhaps by installing display lighting or repositioning other furniture so that the object stands in a space of its own. The strength of a focal point is that it should need very little else surrounding it, so be disciplined and reduce the number of objects in the room, rather than adding more.

Because focal points are so integral to a room, it is hard to decorate first and then find one that fits exactly in terms of size, subject, and style. If, when you are thinking about the space and how you are going to position the furniture, you can see in your mind's eye the place for something dramatic, then carry this image around with you until you find what you are looking for. It should be something you love; a can't-live-without buy, from which the rest of the scheme will evolve.

Although the first view of a room is important, it is necessary to consider other angles, too. Walk around the room, stand and sit, think about how the dynamics of the space change according to where you are. How are you going to arrange objects so that you magnify the strong points of the room while diminishing the weak ones? If, for example, you have your back turned to your chosen focal point when sitting on the sofa, how are you going to create a secondary tableau to provide interest? As you are now at a different eye level, you will have to design something that corresponds to this—perhaps a collection of some sort arranged on a table, or pictures that are stacked against a wall rather than hung.

Take time to think honestly about the objects themselves. Too often we hang on to things out of habit, nostalgia, or laziness. We become so accustomed to seeing certain items every day that in fact we no longer see them at all. Yet why bother to give room in your life to anything you don't absolutely love? Absence makes the heart grow fonder, so if in doubt, pack all the extraneous things away and spend time enjoying your totally blank canvas. If, after a month, you can barely remember what used to be in a certain place, then it is probably time to say goodbye to it for good. Only those items you consciously miss should be put back again.

Remember that there are essentially two reasons for buying objects for the home. The first is because they mean something. If you travel a lot, for example, you may enjoy collecting souvenirs—often beautiful, hand-crafted objects—that remind you of certain locations and occasions. In other words, you are buying for the object itself—not with any decorative scheme in mind. The second way of buying is to decide on a theme, such as a particular color or material—and to make this a pivotal factor in your scheme. It means that shopping trips take on more purpose, as you will be looking for specific shapes, colors, or styles that complement everything else.

There is no right or wrong here, because homes are intensely personal places. However, it is worth recognizing which category you fit and deciding how comfortable you are with that. The first injects a home with character and individuality; the second achieves a more cohesive visual effect. Perhaps it is enough to say that you should at least be confident that everything you buy fits into one of those definitions.

Next, you have to think about how you are going to arrange these objects for the greatest visual impact. If you have identical or similar objects, group these close together so that they become more than the sum of their parts. Decide whether you want a symmetrical or asymmetrical grouping, or whether you are going to include other objects that relate in some way—perhaps through height, form, color, or texture.

Remember the importance of contrast: an arrangement of highly decorative objects will be best appreciated when set against a backdrop of clean, straight lines. A quiet scheme of creams and taupes might benefit from a jolt of red. A narrow alcove might suggest the proportions of a small painting; so, instead, fill it with the biggest mirror you can.

Finally, take time over detailing. Your friends and family might think you are mad to spend hours grouping arrangements of objects or paintings, only to do it again a day later, but the perfectionist in you is a thing to celebrate. Ensuring everything is in alignment are the hallmarks of the unashamed idealist.

OPPOSITE A pair of pomelos suggest the beauty of an old master painting. Their waxy skin and vibrant color have been highlighted here by carefully considered lighting, which brings out their texture to perfection. The wenge tray on which they stand merges quietly into the background

ABOVE A room should comprise many pleasing views, both large and small. This floating shelf is the setting for a contemplative still life, which combines striking black-and-white photography with antique silver boxes, carefully stacked, and a Perspex box of iris leaves. Each object is carefully aligned with the next to achieve Zen-like harmony.

Scenes within a room can be arranged for maximum visual impact. If you have an object that is bold in scale, form, or color, use it as the eye-catching centerpiece of a room. Here, a magnificent bronze head of a horse has been cleverly positioned to create a focal point within this elegant living room, although in fact it is located in the courtyard outside. Commissioning a pedestal of the right height and material is essential to the success of such a piece. The wenge slatted blinds create a dramatic frame around it, adding to the sense of grandeur. These have pale cotton binding tape running down their length, accentuating the lines within the room and forcing the eye forward. Lush greenery on topiary plants in front of the statue and trees behind accentuate the depth of vision. Furniture within the room has also been positioned so as to lead the eye forward, as with the centrally placed wenge table, on which a simple glass bowl of pussy willow and calla lilies is equivalent to visual punctuation. The result is a spectacular tableau built around one strong image.

OPPOSITE The smallest of details are relevant to the success of a scheme. Here, exquisite stitching on a leather chair introduces another layer of texture and pattern.

ABOVE Walls of shelving can be used as striking display areas. Here, the central shelf has been designed to accommodate the television, because often it is better to be bold where home leisure equipment is concerned, rather than attempt to conceal it. Other shelves hold books, stacked aesthetically rather than in conventional rows. Interspersed with these are decorative objects. Stacking black-and-white photography at floor level has the effect of drawing the eye downward from the television toward the more unusual forms of the headrests. Fiber-optic lighting has been inset into shelf edges, adding a witty touch to an otherwise wholly functional piece of furniture.

OPPOSITE Kitchens are often an unexpected source of objects that are decorative as well as functional. These humble glass mixing bowls have been half filled with white sand on which white cattleya orchids lie. The marble table on which they stand makes a visual link with the marble fireplace behind; between them stands a white leather Mies van der Rohe stool with cashmere throw.

ABOVE A white lacquer tray makes the perfect home for miniature water bottles. The table on which they stand is wenge, with a stainless-steel insert running down the center that complements the white metal Venetian blinds at the window.

ABOVE The vertical lines of this taupe-painted cabinet have been intersected by the wooden floor and leather-covered stool, stressing the graphic qualities of the scheme. Inset glass shelves cut out of one panel make the perfect display area for a collection of white ceramic bottles—another example of how very modest objects can be used to decorative effect. The result is calm, harmonious, and soothing to the eye.

PAGE 90 A stack of white towels on a wenge slatted shelf makes an interesting textural play against a limestone floor. Stored at a lower height than is usual, they become part of a pleasing still-life composition.

PAGE 91 The interior of this bathroom cabinet has been lit to create an unexpected display area. A line of empty bottles etched across this backdrop looks beautiful in its simplicity, but can also be used for more practical purposes.

Walls are often underestimated in design, seen only as boundaries between one area and another. However, they are also backdrops for items—both functional and decorative—and can be used to layer up interest. The limestone wall and work surface of this bathroom are not only quietly beautiful, but also inviting to the touch and extremely durable. The lines of the shaving mirror create a strong form against this neutral canvas.

ABOVE The curve of a television screen cuts across the outline of the skylight above, creating an intriguing sequence of lines and arcs.

BELOW The side view of a cotton-covered chair with vertically stacked cushions shows a similar effect of rounded edges intersecting the lines of the linen draperies. Horizontal banding at the bottom adds an extra visual twist.

OPPOSITE Bathrooms are often overlooked in terms of creating aesthetically pleasing scenes, but this limestone design is used as the backdrop for a fabulous combination of objects. The seductive curve of the 1960s Panton chair in fiberglass makes an unexpected setting for a still life of vellum books and ivory boxes. The color and texture of the vellum are picked up in the taupe-colored towels on the rail behind.

ABOVE AND OPPOSITE Cushions are the ideal way of combining textures for contrast. These carefully stacked examples are made of leather with velvet, leather with voile, and simple cotton, perfectly complementing the ostrich headboard and sheer curtains.

PAGES 98–99 The way in which each element in a space relates to all the others is key to the visual success of a room. The Zen-like atmosphere of this calm living room is evident not only in its pale colors but also through the way shapes are echoed, from the black-and-white photographs of roses, to the linen seats below, to the two-by-three arrangement of roses in glass bowls on the table. A bird's-eye view of these shows pussy willow twisted around the circumference with a rose placed in the center.

REFLECTIONS AND ECHOES

What I strive for above all else when decorating is absolute harmony. An interior should not be composed of a series of disparate elements, but should consist of carefully considered ideas that vibrate throughout each room. Rooms may have different characters that accentuate their separateness or, alternatively, melt into each other, so continuing this feeling of reverberation. At best, an entire house will be visually in tune on every level from basement to attic.

The reflections and echoes of a room are a way of achieving this harmony. However, reflections have three interpretations for the decorator, each of them contributing to the overall design of a room. The first is literal: the idea of introducing reflective surfaces that then magnify an effect. Mirrors are the most obvious way of doing this, but they are not the only option. There are now wallpaper and paint finishes that have reflective qualities, as well as textural ones. Metallic papers, for example, not only create interest on a wall but, when combined with good lighting and interesting objects, create the most beautiful and subtle reflections and shadows throughout the space.

Glossy surfaces, too, bring added interest to a room. Juxtapose them with a contrasting matte texture, so highlighting their individual qualities. A stainless-steel runner down a wenge table is a striking example of how a reflective surface interplays with a dense one, as is a satin band around a velvet cushion. Glass furniture or accessories are the most obvious ways to introduce a reflective surface to a scheme, but consider mixing plain with opaque or etched glass for a more contemporary look.

The second interpretation is more intellectual: the idea of reflecting on a room and its success from a design point of view. It is about taking time to think carefully about what has been created and whether there are improvements still to be made. So often people make a good job of transforming a room decoratively, but then fail to put in the last five percent of work—the detailing. Finishing a room well is one of the hardest tasks, yet it does make the difference between something that looks amateur and a professional result. Be critical: try to take the vantage point of someone walking in for the first time. Pause to contemplate whether you have achieved everything you wanted to in the space.

The third interpretation is about sending out reflections through a room, metaphorically speaking; and this is closely related to the idea of harmony. It centers on the notion that colors, textures, forms, and lines should all work together in perfect balance. It means that there should be a reason for everything that has been chosen and where it has been placed. You must train your eye to focus on what is there and make confident decisions about what works and what does not. A scheme might appear very simple—neutral colors, clean lines—but that might disguise the care that has been taken to make sure everything is in perfect alignment. The line of a rug, for example, might reflect that of a banquette. A row of ceramic bowls on a mantelpiece might link subtly to the round face of a clock on a cabinet. This ability to analyze shape, scale, and line—and to play on it—is integral to the way I decorate.

Having thought about reflections, now consider echoes. The echoes of a room are the subliminal messages that certain objects, fabrics, furniture shapes, or colors send out. You might, for example, bring nature into your scheme by including organic objects or simple arrangements of leaves, twigs, and flowers. You might suggest the ocean through a color scheme or bowls of pebbles. You might inject a note of glamor from the past with swathes of Fortuny fabric or black-and-white photographic images. This is a very subtle level of decorating, but can be the way of designing something really special. Suggestion is a powerful force, so remember that understatement is the key. One perfectly placed object is enough, so don't feel tempted to overdo it. Gone are the days of heavily themed rooms: the contemporary approach to decorating demands a more restrained approach.

Start by making the space as pure and uncluttered as possible. Now take one object you really love, something with eye-catching form. Place it where it can be seen to best effect; but now really observe its shape and lines. Is there a way of repeating these in some way? It might be that you have chosen to position it against the window, in which case a curtain, drapery, or shade may offer the potential to make a visual link. Or perhaps you can find something of a similar style, but on a much smaller scale. If so, is there a way of arranging this object nearby, on a mantelpiece or side table perhaps? Once you have your starting point, it should be possible to build on it.

Finally, make sure you maintain this disciplined frame of mind in your approach to the whole room. Do not introduce other items that stop the flow from object to object. Remember that all these gentle visual links are a way of achieving a cohesive whole.

When choosing furniture that will be used on an everyday basis, such as seating, remember that comfort must be high on your list of priorities. As far as design is concerned, it is best to opt for something that has pleasing form and offers some flexibility—a sense of timelessness is also an advantage. These graceful dining chairs are covered in simple unbleached muslin, which suits their clean lines and painted frames perfectly. However, they can also be transformed with the use of simple slipcovers that pull over the top, creating an entirely different look according to mood, season, or occasion.

LEFT AND BELOW The milky blues and slate grays of this beautifully dressed table create a scene as cool as winter. Mirrors are the conventional companion to fireplaces, but here textured silver wallpaper makes an interesting alternative while still introducing a reflective quality. Organic shapes, such as the collection of coral and the swathes of pleated table linen, make a visual play against the underlying structure found in rows of ceramic eggs and boxes of upright twigs. A scrim runner over the muslin cloth emphasizes the sense of order.

105

OPPOSITE Consider how each item in a room relates to the shapes and textures around it. Here, the intricate surface of a shagreen console table has been echoed in a collection of beads displayed in a silvered glass bowl. The blues, grays, and greens of the composition are reminiscent of the sea, so that at first glance the beads resemble shells and pebbles gathered from the shore.

ABOVE Pearl buttons displayed on a white lacquer tray catch light and color, as though they were bubbles in water. Conventionally used to embellish other objects, they have been arranged here in isolation so that their own beauty can be fully appreciated.

A close-up of the view shown on page 104 throws the spotlight onto the fabulous wealth of textures. The organic form of coral is so strong that very little of it is needed to have an impact within a room. Here its sculptural qualities have been accentuated by the uneven surface of the silver wallpaper and the smoothness of the marble fireplace. The black-and-white image behind echoes the sensuous shape of the coral arms.

Roses have been synonymous with beauty for centuries. Here they have been given a contemporary twist by submerging them in Perspex vases rather than displaying them—as is traditional—long-stemmed and tall. The trick of producing such an effect for yourself is to cut the roses very short and place them in the vase before adding water. Trickle it in slowly and stop the moment the rose begins to move; otherwise it will not sit perfectly. Seen in this way, they appear to be framed, frozen in time and space. Note, too, how displaying the roses individually encourages one to focus on their individual characteristics. Their creamy color and silky texture need no other accompaniment.

ABOVE The reflective surfaces of a row of silver teapots highlights them in a room dominated by wenge furniture.

OPPOSITE A trio of floating shelves underlit with fiber-optic lighting creates a calm, contemplative focal point in this restrained living room. The creamy leather upholstery and bolster cushion of the modern chaise-longue blend with the other subdued colors.

BELOW The interiors of drawers and cabinets should be as carefully considered as the exteriors.

The addition of one material into a scheme can greatly influence the overall style or mood. Wood, for example, might be regarded as too traditional a choice for furniture, but can be introduced through artifacts that reveal its textural beauty. This collection of African headrests creates wonderful sculptural shapes against the taupe-painted wall. Floating shelves have been chosen because they are unobtrusive and do not detract from what is displayed on them. The richness of the wood contrasts perfectly with the contemporary elegance of the slim silvered glass lamp. This combination is a perfect example of how antique objects can be juxtaposed with modern ones to powerful effect.

OPPOSITE Candles are a decorating essential, not just because they cast such a soft light but because they are also a way of introducing scent. A sculpted candle looks fabulous when seen up close next to a waxy palm leaf.

ABOVE A collection of free-form glass vases inspired by the shapes of pebbles brings robust form, ripples of color, and exciting reflective texture to this otherwise tranquil living room. Propped on floating shelves above is a group of white-framed photographs depicting roses. The organic shapes of the glass contrast in an interesting way with this linear arrangement.

OPPOSITE In this wenge-and-limestone bathroom a gloriously textured wooden artifact creates an effective focal point.

ABOVE A textured wall and wenge dado provide the backdrop for a linen-covered headboard and bedspread. Silk pillows inject opulence into the scheme, while a row of dark blue hyacinth bulbs on a bed of shingle placed on the wenge table introduce a flash of color.

BELOW Two huge glass vases in which Liberty amaryllis are submerged echo the lines of ceiling-to-floor panels in the background.

PAGE 120 Track lighting has been inset into this ceiling, making it possible to achieve some spectacular effects.

PAGE 121 A pebble floor is a fabulous way of creating contrast and making texture central to a decorative scheme.

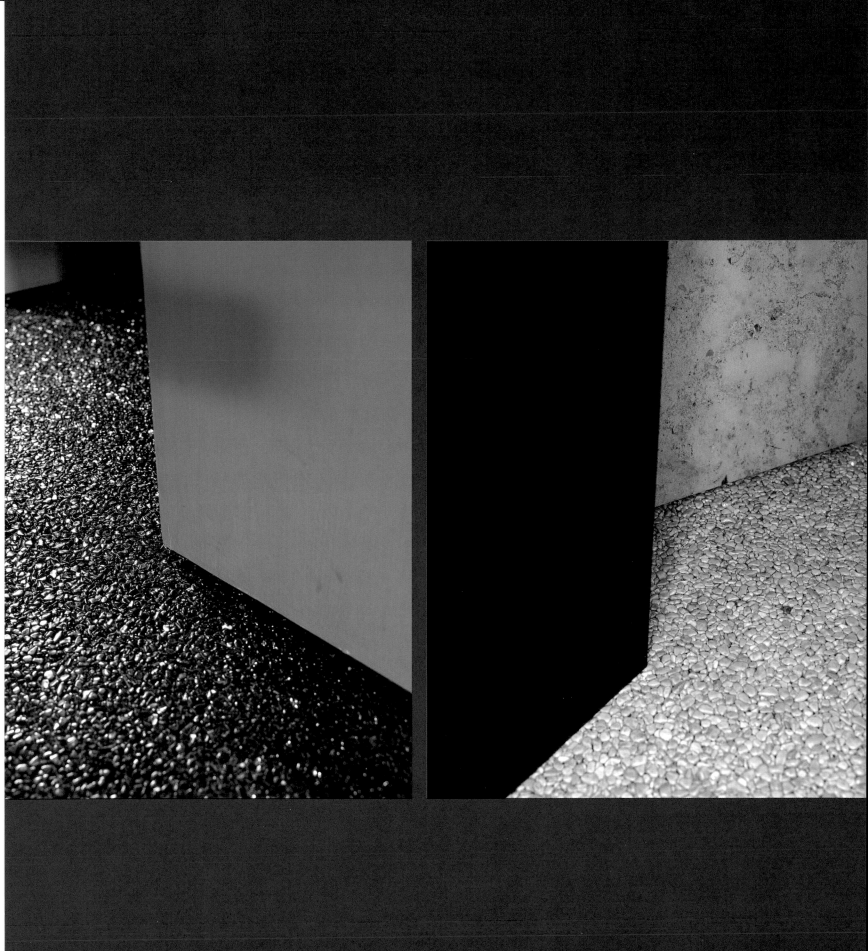

This simply decorated living room brings together many key design strategies. The textured wall, for example, incorporates a runner effect that stresses the underlying grid structure of the space. The roughness of this, juxtaposed with the smoothness of adjacent flat-painted walls, is interesting both to the eye and to the touch. The monochrome scheme combines a dark wenge floor and table and simple linen upholstery, with only the sharp green of cocoa leaves to inject vivid color into the room. Contrast is evident not only in textural choices—such as the sheer curtains and wooden artifact—but in the way that such a traditional fireplace has been dressed in a contemporary look, with a trio of small ceramic bowls and silver beakers placed at each end of the mantelpiece. A group of three Perspex pots on the table echoes these arrangements. The expressive curve of the leaf is striking against the order apparent elsewhere.

ABOVE The stainless-steel runner inlaid down this wenge table is a natural backdrop for glass vases filled with green variegated leaves. Submerging them in this way makes it possible to appreciate fully their lacy texture and glorious color. White hilophapos orchids resting on a wreath of pussy willow complete the picture.

OPPOSITE A close-up of the cocoa leaf seen on the mantelpiece on page 125 shows the interplay between its waxy stripes and the roughness of the textured wall.

PAGE 128 A petal-shaped silver bowl on a wenge table makes a fabulous display vessel for mother-of-pearl buttons. The amount of light each surface attracts contributes to the dramatic effect.

PAGE 129 Lights set into the bathroom wall near the floor

OPPOSITE One strong material is enough to set the atmospheric tone of a room. This guest bathroom has a carved slate basin and special-effect-painted walls. The density of these has been balanced with a wenge-framed mirror. On the slate worktop is a Perspex box filled with shingle and hyacinth bulbs, which again bring together the qualities of matte and gloss.

ABOVE The base of a wenge-framed mirror is seen set against a painted radiator cover on which stand three horn beakers. These not only introduce a textural dimension but also inject pattern into the scheme.

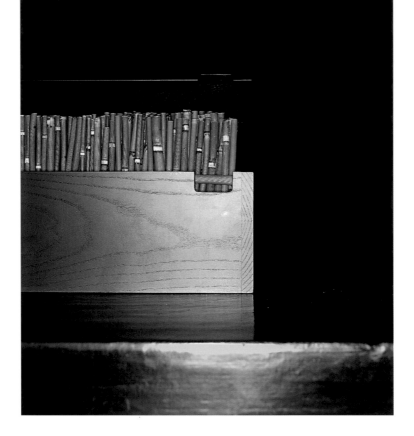

ABOVE Think laterally when considering how natural objects might be displayed within a room. Here a wenge box has been packed with snake-grass to spectacular effect. The wenge table and linen curtains provide a neutral canvas for the arrangement.

OPPOSITE Sticks of bamboo have been tied together to create a decorative frame for a ceramic plate. The granite surface and textured wall make an ideal base for the reflective surfaces of the glass under plate, side plate, and coaster.

PAGE 134 Even natural objects can be embellished for interest. Here artichokes have been wrapped in coir string to increase their textural significance. A simple lacquer bowl is the perfect foil for such elaborate leaves.

PAGE 135 Backlit floating shelves above the slate work surface of a city kitchen are used as a display area for a row of identical white ceramic bowls. Three moss balls above make an eye-catching focal point, while baking trays of greenery continue the color theme.

OPPOSITE An intimate dining area has been created by using linen panels to separate off one corner of a room. The wenge table and chairs are extra high, stressing the vertical lines of the room. These are further accentuated by the tall lamp and the gold runners that fall to the floor on each side. Horizontal widths of bark balance the proportions of the space and make interesting vessels for food. ABOVE The space between this wenge radiator cover and the wenge mirror frame makes an ideal backdrop for a row of glass vases. Orchids wrapped in leaves have a Japanese-style beauty on which the eye can rest.

ABOVE The accordion-fold action of this antique chain mirror sets up a sequence of fabulous reflections in this entrance hall, fooling the eye into believing the space is bigger than it is. Plain woolen upholstery has been teamed with a magnificent dévoré cushion, while an industrial wall lamp has been juxtaposed with an ornate glass-based one. The shagreen table, inlaid chinoiserie boxes, and Chinese trunk accentuate the mood of restrained opulence.

OPPOSITE A wenge lamp with linen shade casts dramatic lighting over a chair upholstered in Alcantara suede with matching cushions.

LEFT A quiet corner for reading has been created in this elegant bedroom, with a lamp carefully positioned over a crewelwork-upholstered chair. Wenge-and-mirror wardrobes across the width of the room increase the feeling of space, while horizontal bands on the linen draperies also accentuate the proportions of the room. An antiquarian clay figure on a wenge radiator cover is positioned for maximum visual impact.

BELOW Sheer curtains and linen Roman shades have been used together here to create interesting effects of light and shadow. These have been emphasized by placing a semi-translucent philodendron leaf in a Perspex box against the window. Its luminous finish contrasts with the wenge desk on which the only other object is a pencil pot.

OPPOSITE Concealed spaces should be thought about as carefully as those that are on display. The door of this mirrored bathroom cabinet has a square shape cut out of its panel, through which a light shines.

ABOVE Floating shelves lit with fiber-optic lighting create a chic display area in a calm living room. A row of identical glass bowls filled with pussy willow and rose blooms holds the eye. The arc each bowl makes is in contrast to the rigid lines of the room.

ABOVE A painted slatted door has been used to screen off a television when not in use.

OPPOSITE ABOVE Traditional balusters have been replaced here with ones made of glass. The lustrous surface of these makes an interesting interplay against the density of the wood. The way they catch the light also introduces an additional layer of beauty into the room.

OPPOSITE BELOW Here, linen panels have replaced conventional doors in a dressing room. A slim wenge table at the far end is the setting for a dramatic wooden artifact, while the wenge-and-linen stool can be used for seating or the folding of clothes.

OPPOSITE **This vermilion-and-taupe drapery has been made out of two colorways in the same wool, joined together to form a horizontal band. The richness of the tones and the boldness of the stripe create a striking effect.**

ABOVE **Plain linen pillows have been embellished here with horizontal bands of scarlet iridescent silk. This treatment accentuates the linear structure of the room and is a way of introducing a touch of opulence to an otherwise restrained scheme.**

BELOW **A wenge cabinet with nickel handles makes the perfect foil for three antique match strikers. The shape of these is surprisingly modern and sets up interesting contrasts of form and texture against the furniture.**

ABOVE This breathtaking image shows a Perspex tray of crimson dahlias against a wenge table. It reveals that the simplest of arrangements can produce the most spectacular effects if only the imagination is harnessed effectively. Using flowers of a single color in this way not only creates dramatic impact but also throws the spotlight onto their individual shapes and structures.

PAGE 150 A view through linen panels shows a different view of the bed seen on page 71. The concrete base and ostrich headboard remain the same, but here a rich red velvet runner, charcoal-gray satin eiderdown, and gray flannel pillows create a warmer mood.

PAGE 151 A close-up of the red velvet runner shows how it can also make a sensuous base for plates of food.

Now that scent has been recognized as a powerful influence on the ambience of a house, incense is no longer the domain of teenage bedrooms. Often stronger than candles or flowers, it is ideal for rooms where you want to create a warm, sensuous atmosphere—particularly at night. Here a marble base has been used, which allows the incense sticks to become another linear ingredient of the scheme.

OPPOSITE The clean curve of a black leather-and-chrome chaise longue has been positioned to cut across the linear form of a linen Roman shade.

ABOVE A mushroom-shaped floor-standing lamp in metal.

BELOW A pair of Chinese chairs make an unexpected accompaniment to the graphic lines of a painted cabinet.

PUBLISHING DIRECTOR Anne Furniss

CREATIVE DIRECTOR Mary Evans

TEXT Helen Chislett

PHOTOGRAPHY Thomas Stewart

STYLING Samantha Todhunter

DESIGN Jim Smith

PRODUCTION Vincent Smith, Sarah Tucker

First published in the United States of America
in 2001 by
Rizzoli International Publications, Inc.
300 Park Avenue South
New York, NY 10010

First published in Great Britain
in 2001 by
Quadrille Publishing Limited
Alhambra House
27-31 Charing Cross Road
London WC2H 0LS

ISBN 0-8478-2419-5
Library of Congress 2001092077

Printed in and bound in Germany

PHOTOGRAPHIC ACKNOWLEDGMENTS
The author and publisher would like to thank the following people and organizations for
lending items for photography. Page numbers indicate where to find the photographs in which
these items appear:

Aero (tel: 011 44 20 7221 1950; 011 44 20 7351 0511) 95
Annick Richardson at Shanxi (tel: 011 44 20 7498 7611) 138
Babylon (tel: 011 44 20 7376 7255) 22,39,71,106,114,149
CA1 (tel: 011 44 20 7611 5200) 149
C. Best (tel: 011 44 20 7720 2306) 104–5, 109
Ciancimino (tel: 011 44 20 7730 9950) 33, 34,55,138
Coexistence (tel: 011 44 20 7354 8817) 38
Bodo Sperlein (tel: 011 44 20 7633 9413) 105
David Champion (tel: 011 44 20 7727 6016) 104–5, 114
Egg (tel: 011 44 20 7235 9315) 135
Evertrading (tel: 011 44 20 8878 4050) 76
Fired Earth (tel: 011 44 1295 812 088) 38, 74, 114
General Trading Company (tel: 011 44 20 7943 5303) 25, 48, 71, 92, 93, 116, 131
Guinevere (tel: 011 44 20 7736 2917) 25, 32, 40, 54, 55, 71, 83 113
Habitat (tel: 011 44 20 7255 2545) 88, 104–5
Hilary Batstone Antiques (tel: 011 44 20 7730 5335) 138
Interiors Bis (tel: 011 44 20 7838 1104) 59, 82, 113, 132
Jane Sacchi Linen (tel: 011 44 20 7838 1001) 40, 68, 71, 150
Kate Hume Glass (tel: 011 31 20 620 3030) 117
Kelaty (tel: 011 44 20 8903 9998) 34
Michael Hoppen Gallery (tel: 011 44 20 7352 3649) 14, 38, 60, 61, 83, 99, 113
Muji (tel: 011 44 20 7436 1779) 1, 56, 63, 67, 71, 72, 83, 104–5, 110, 113, 130
Nom (tel: 011 44 20 7584 4158) 12, 89, 104–5, 134
Pickett (tel: 011 44 20 7823 5638) 58
R.J. Norris Beds (tel: 011 44 20 7274 5306) 71
Selfridges (tel: 011 44 20 7629 1234) 53, 76
Silent Gliss (tel: 011 44 1843 863571) 33, 71, 150
Space (tel: 011 44 20 7229 6533) 39
The Cube (tel: 011 44 20 7938 2244) 71, 152
Viaduct (tel: 011 44 20 7278 8456) 99
William Yeoward (tel: 011 44 20 7351 5454) 25
Wojnowski (tel: 011 44 20 7584 5353) 99
Wolfin Textiles (tel: 011 44 20 7636 4949) 102–3, 104–5
Yeoward South (tel: 011 44 20 7498 4811) 12, 16, 44, 104–5, 118, 147
Yoma (tel 011 44 7957 881 926) 40, 150

If you have any queries, please call Samantha Todhunter at 011 44 20 7243 1065